BLACK
DRUM

BLACK DRUM

poems by ENID SHOMER

The UNIVERSITY *of*
ARKANSAS PRESS
Fayetteville
1997

Copyright 1997 by Enid Shomer

Manufactured in the United States of America

01   00   99   98   97   5   4   3   2   1

Designed by Alice Gail Carter

☺   The paper used in this publication meets
the minimum requirements of the American
National Standard for Permanence of Paper
for Printed Library Materials   z39.48-1984.

Library of Congress Cataloging-in-Publication Data
Shomer, Enid.
    Black drum : poems / Enid Shomer.
      p.   cm.
    ISBN 1-55728-494-6 (cloth : alk. paper). —
    ISBN 1-55728-497-0 (paper : alk. paper)
    I. Title.
    PS3569.H5783B57   1997
    811'.54—dc21   97-6878
                                CIP

for Levent

ACKNOWLEDGMENTS

These poems were written with the support of grants from the National Endowment for the Arts as well as the Florida Arts Council.

I am grateful to the editors of the following magazines where these poems first appeared, sometimes in slightly different form:

The Atlantic: "Global Aphasia"

Boulevard: "'Thérèse Dreaming'"

Epiphany: The Ogalala Review: "'The Lonely Ones'"

Field: "Thistles," "Articulos Religiosos"

FORUM: The Magazine of the Florida Humanities Council: "Into the Land of Flowers"

Georgia Review: "Hermit Crab"

Hurakan: "For the Women of the All-Female Bookkeeping Department at H. G. Smithy's"

Kalliope: "A Floridian Swimming in Brooklyn"

The Kenyon Review: "The Separation," "For My Sister" (under the title "Depth of Field"), "The Gene," and "For the Stillness" (under the title "Refreshed Apollo")

The Massachusetts Review: "Table for Four," "Snoop," "The Mystery of My Father's Cleanliness"

The New Criterion: "Cadillac," "Seeing Cousins after Many Years"

Ontario Review: "At Freud's House"

Parnassus: Poetry in Review: "My Friend Who Sings before Breakfast"

Poetry: "Black Drum," "Elegy and Rant for My Father," "In the Viennese Style," "Passive Resistance," "Letter Home from Brooklyn"

Prairie Schooner: "Life List," "Theater of Dreams"

Southern Poetry Review: "Notes from the Sketchbook of Gustav Klimt"

Tikkun: "King David Memorial Gardens," "I See My Father in the Afterlife"

•   •   •

"Passive Resistance" was selected for *The Best American Poetry 1996* (New York: Scribners, 1996).

"My Friend Who Sings before Breakfast" won the Randall Jarrell Poetry Prize.

"Into the Land of Flowers," was commissioned for the Florida Humanities Council project "Making Florida Home."

"Global Aphasia" appears in the anthology *Articulations: The Body and Illness in Poetry* (Iowa City: University of Iowa Press, 1994) and in the American Speech, Hearing and Language Association's anthology *The First Yes* (Washington, D.C.: Dryad Press, 1996).

"Vigil without Words" first appeared in *I've Always Meant to Tell You: Letters to Our Mothers* (New York: Pocket Books, 1997).

CONTENTS

*If I don't burn, if you don't burn
how will the darkness ever turn
into light?*

—NAZIM HIKMET

Cadillac

Imagine my squat, blue-eyed Russian
grandfather, a stogie in his fist, a Stetson

on his head, a silk suit precisely vented,
ordered from a rabbi with a sideline and friends

in Hong Kong. Imagine his voyage here alone
at thirteen, the sea like a pasture of fescue combed

by the wind and him hiding most of the time in that carousel
of piss and vomit. Imagine the babies crying, the charred smell

of food cooked in steerage, the dark knots
of men smoking and gambling. Did they hate

Jews, too? Imagine him on Ellis Island with his wild Slavic face
and the space between his shoulders that always

itched, puffing out his chest for the doctors.
One deep breath puts his name on the roster

Americanized—the *ik* chopped off of Magazinik
to make Magazine, a word he understands means a quick

book. He has no notion yet of luxury or charity, of leather
sofas or engraved plaques or dinners in honor

of. These will come after ice cream vending
and carpentry thin his voice and thicken his hands,

after he loses every cent in the Depression, and begins
his big ventures—Fort Stevens, Brandywine,

1000 Connecticut Avenue, that soaring granite address
that was like the White House for us,

a sparkling tower where he sat like a prince
thirty levels above the polished marble dance

floor of the lobby. O once more let him watch the phony
wrestlers on TV, his shoulders lurching with each throw.

I want to see him sop pleasure again from a bowl
with a heel of bread, dipping and slurping, his whole

face slick with broth and steam. And the deck
of nudie cards he kept hidden in the top right desk

drawer, redheads with tits like roses. And the slow
way he rolled his "l"s across his tongue, as if savoring fish roe.

I remember how short he was behind the wheel of his prize—
they called them Jew canoes in those days—

how joyfully he packed us in on Sundays, plowing down the road,
letting the big car drift across the center line, like a parade.

Table for Four

His name's Sollie, the customer in front of me
with walnut-shell cheeks and round Italian eyes.
I'm holding onto my mother, frail on her tripod cane.
It's Saturday night on the Gold Coast, Mario's
is the third restaurant we've tried and the line is half
an hour long. *Go ahead*, Sollie says,

after five minutes, *Just take your mother inside.*
The line seethes like a hornet's nest at a whiff of smoke.
He points to the pick-up counter where an old man
with a walker is parked, his hair singeing distance
from pizza pans and bowls of hot pasta fagioli.
I leave her there on a chair. Waitresses with steaming

trays flow around her, like rapids around a rock.
I return to the line, to the old Italian with yellowed
fingers, hands enlarged by a trade—carpentry,
I'd guess. I stare through the glass doors at the silent space
between my mother and me, like watching the spot where someone
has drowned. She looks small and lost, as she always looked

at dinner, where my father loomed, a cyclops
with his single eye on his food and his breath a scorching wind.
We were both children then. Neither one could save
the other those nights the table was pressed at my ribs
like a weapon and I imagined being sliced in half
when he pushed against it to stand . . . .

Sollie says I'll get

a table for four, Honey. Wait inside with your mother.
That's when he tells me his name and I tell him mine
and I notice how much he resembles my father, who's home dying
of emphysema and a foul soul—same swarthy skin
and wavy hair, same thin body that clothes hang from
like makeshift drapes pinned at a window. *You can eat*

with my wife and me. Did you ever feel you'd faint
from kindness? I thank him and go inside. When a waitress
rigs us a table near the phone, I pluck them
from the line. He smiles shyly, as if I'd asked him
for a date. It is flirtation between us.
Even though he's old, maybe seventy-five, I want him

to love me. I think I remind him of the dark girls
in the town of Publo where his people, all shepherds,
own half a mountain. *There,* his thick finger touching
my placemat map. He's wearing the navy wool cap
of Tuscany. When his ziti comes, he shovels a meatball
onto my plate and tells me *Taste, taste how Italian*

it is. I am a vegetarian, but I eat it
gratefully, I eat what the father gives.
Mother, who hasn't met anyone new since her stroke, talks
to his wife. Giselda's crucifix is so huge
that when she breathes, fingers and toes squirm against
her peasant blouse, its gray like a querulous sky.

At home, Mother, a sparkle of gold bangles and bleached
blonde hair, will talk about how plain Giselda
was—no make-up, faded brown cardigan—but now

she chatters and fusses, hurrying like a bird before
you cover the cage at night. Sollie and I chat
about Firenze's fragrant soups, how many years

he's been in the States, how he found this place on his way
home from the track. *The track*, where my father lived
his only life and which might as well have been heroin tracks
on a user. My father, who's home dying of loss, his lungs
empty as pockets turned inside out. Each time I look
at Sollie, I see my father's face without the sneer,

without the temper sputtering from his lips. He smokes
and drinks coffee all through the meal, enjoying
himself the way my father never could. He says,
You're a good daughter, meaning I take my mother out,
but I pretend he means to him, a good daughter
to him. Then he and Giselda stand, saying they'll be back

in a minute, and he secretly pays our bill. I rise
from my seat when I realize what he's done, but he's out
the door and I'm moving in slow motion, as slow as any
healing, and Mother wants to know why he paid and why
I'm crying and why I'm coming undone and I am the wisp
of smoke that hangs in the forest air and he is the fire

that made me and has already moved on.

Elegy and Rant for My Father

He grew up poor, believing only in luck.
His mother ran numbers; his father cut

hair. Hence the parimutuel tickets
embedded in the acrylic seat of his toilet,

the horses everywhere—nodding from chains on his chest,
petit-pointed jumping across his vest

buttons, wreathed in diamonds in a tiny
winner's circle that revolved on his pinky

ring. In old age he walked with his head hung
forward and down, as if a horseshoe were slung

around his neck. O heart like a fist! Nine
professional bouts as a bantamweight and then

his glass jaw shattered and all his promises broke.
When he was young and Miami was young, he worked

for the mob. Hair slicked back with sweet
pomades, he paid off deputies, placed bets.

O heart of pure gristle! He once paid a nickel
to sleep standing up in a Chicago flophouse, his satchel

strapped to his leg. He lacked ambition, waited
for things to break the way a fisherman waits

for the tide to turn and learns to love the quiet
spells between strikes, and learns to equate

his failures with his thrills. O heart like a serpent
knotted on itself! He was angry, he was ignorant

and nothing—not good suits or manicures
or flush nights or his wife's money—could secure

his signature on a check. Bad mortgage risk,
he was cursed and he cursed, his tongue a tusk

that gored you and left you bleeding in public
and still you covered for him. O heart like a hook!

He made you feel like a slut if your bra strap
showed, if you laughed too much or came home happy.

O heart like a cavern where you cried and kissed
at the darkness and mistook the echo of your own voice

for his! We buried him fourteen months later
than the doctor predicted. At the track that last year

with a wheelchair and oxygen tank: eighty-five pounds of hope
in stinking checkered pants and a baseball cap.

Adrenaline of the long shot, heart of an ox,
they said. At the grave, the lowering cord knocked

the Star of David off the coffin into the earth
and it was fitting because he was Jewish only by birth

and food and Yiddish joke. Still, they washed
his body devoutly and wrapped him head to toe in a wish—

a puffy white shroud like a cocoon where his last gamble,
a blue and white prayer shawl barely visible

through the gauze, lay like the colorful tips
of wings that would unfold in the next life.

Global Aphasia

It's like a two-way street, the hospital speech
therapist explains, drawing lanes with arrows

and curves. Information swerves in through the ears;
replies arrive in the mouth. The brain is the driver.

"Okay okay okay," Mother answers without delay
when asked about the food, her health, this task.

This "automatic response," a kind of static, relieves
the silence she emotes like a high-frequency note

of distress. "Brush your . . . ?" "Suitcase," she rushes to fill
in the blank, shaking her head as you would to free the ink

in a ballpoint pen. "Tie your . . . ?" Mother's eyes roll.
"Suitcase?" she pleads. At the root of "perseveration," the name

for this odd repeating of words, is the word "persevere,"
that hopeful bird which sits on my chest with its head

snaked under a wing and its talons digging in as she shakes
more and more suitcases loose from her mind. One shines

on her finger, one barks like a dog. O singer with your one-word
song, you knew I was there but not for how long, so all

day you conjured up luggage, all afternoon you lured my bags
from the thicket of thought and picked at the locks of my visit.

Into the Land of Flowers

Where are you going? the relatives asked Grand-
ma Min and Grandpa Alex in Baltimore. To a slab
of sand with mosquitoes and Indians? To pan gold
from the swamps? They lit out for Florida
anyway, valises and crockery crammed in their model-
T. The year was nineteen twenty-six.

Immigrants from Europe, they'd survived six
pogroms (though all her life Min's grandiose
carriage and pretensions were modeled
on the royalty who sent the Slavic
mobs). Paradise gleamed to the south: Florida's
fish free for the catching, golden

fruits and opportunities, the fluted gold
hem of its land, sun blaring like a sax-
ophone in the sky. Tourists with florid
faces needed beauticians and barbers, grand
hairdos to match the sea's marcelles. Alex laved
them with the straight razor. Min modeled

perms in her shop where dryers the hot pink of motel
signs stirred the air. She reached for the gold
ring at the ponies—ran numbers, a small black slab
of a notebook always in her pocket. It was a sick-
ness she passed on to my father. How many grand
did she lose to that sport that held out hope then floored

you with loss by less than a nose? In Florida
they stayed, though their skin grew mottled

with cancer from too much sun and their grand
dream thinned to a balcony overlooking The Golden
Shoe, a bar with drinks called "Thong Bikini" and "Sex
on the Beach." Their fishing holes slabbed

over with cement, they hooked into condos, America's lab-
oratory of old age, those white stands of manmade flora.
Land of Flowers, that's what Florida means—the suc-
culent gardenia with its rusty edge and creamy middle,
the heat and hope that set them adrift like golden
pollen with schemes illegal and grand.

My grandparents' progeny spread through Florida like roots
through concrete slab, like veins of gold. Gone since the sixties,
they lie beneath this remodeled landscape, natives at last.

Seeing Cousins after Many Years

It's their eyes you notice first:
mostly blue and mottled
like the aggies of childhood.
There are firsts, seconds, thirds, once
and twice removed and more
distant still and still
somehow your blood, your history:
Cousin Lana, now fifty-two, who hired a hypnotist
for her sweet sixteen party
(himself a distant cousin, dead now
of an overdose). You remember the fixed
smile of dolls in her hands, rollers
tunneling through her hair, the early
reports about sex. Now she says
her husband is dead—nearly a year.
Eleven hundred miles away, the family
network full of holes, you hadn't heard.

Around the room you count eighteen,
some as skittish as if they stood
on rungs of ladders leaned
against the walls and weren't coming down
for anything.

Later, facing east, toward Jerusalem,
the rabbi lights the candle
that will burn a week for the deceased.
You exchange addresses with a few,
cry with them for the definition
of growing up that means to go

away, for the cliché that death is
what brings this bittersweetness
to you over platters of turkey
and tongue and pastrami and dip
and bottles of schnapps.
The cousins' shy and aging and mostly blue
eyes shine all around the room, jewels
in a giant family scatter pin
spread across this night like the stars
you wished on wildly as a girl,
knowing your words would never reach them.

Snoop

At fifteen, I pawed through his nightstand,
the foil-wrapped rubbers like melting coins.
Now, while mother's in the hospital,
what am I looking for, drawer after drawer?
Something that hugged his body, something
he loved—one of his Mafiosi sweaters with suede
inserts down the chest, the soft armor of animal
influence instead of steel. Always cold,
he groused alone in overheated rooms,
the racing form, his crystal ball,
a-blur with misguessed *perfectas*.

The rabbi aghast, this is how
we laid him down in Virginia
in that giant drawer:
adorned with the horse
jewelry he might have bequeathed us,
family pictures scattered over his body.
On top of the cheesecloth shroud,
our faces seeped like wounds,
while beneath, his receded
into a glacier, the block of coldness
from which he was born.

Desk, dresser, closet—nothing is left,
though weeks after his death
a teller reached through the grille
and counted off some of his heartbeats
into my palm. Afterwards, I hurried
to my car the way he hurried

to place bets—walking, then loping,
freed for a moment from the earth's pull,
floating like the tickets
the loser discards, a heavy
confetti.

Theater of Dreams

Let objects stand for people. Talk only to possessions, not those who possess you.
—INSTRUCTIONS FOR A JUNGIAN EXERCISE

The dream begins in her childhood, deep
in the basement of the house. Now we each take a role.
It's the objects that speak in this drama from sleep:

one person plays the cement floor, another the heap
of clutter that stands for her father—mostly old tools.
The dream begins in her childhood, deep

in her father's arms. She remembers the shrugged-off hope
in his shoulders, his body stiff as his levels and rules.
It's the objects that speak. In this drama from sleep

the floor says *I'm turning to marble* when she weeps.
The thrown shoe, the shouting, the strap hung on a nail—
the dream begins in her childhood. *Deep*

enough now, says the floor, *I'm shining with grief.*
She hugs herself, sensing her bones like braille.
It's the objects that speak in this drama. *From sleep*

you spin a thousand selves, says the clutter, *to keep*
the promises he broke. Now unwind the spool
of dreams. Begin in childhood, deep
in the objects that speak in this drama. From sleep.

King David Memorial Gardens

I went to help put my father
in the ground, the way you lock
something in a box
but don't throw away the key.
I went to see that he was really
gone, that the cruelty
would turn simple and green,
that he would at last receive
the riches of the rain and be rendered
unharmable and harmless—cut
by a mower blade and not bleed
and not warp the steel.

I See My Father in the Afterlife

There's a cloud wrapped around him
like a toga or swaddling—a uniform

that denotes the rank of a slave who barely
escaped hell. When he pares

his nails, here on earth it sleets.
When he curls his toes, the wind tramps its feet

through the trees. Tornadoes brew in his ear.
In hell, he could have joined friends. Here,

he must serve the ones he lied to
and stole from. He must smile

as he lowers trays of Turkish Delight.
He never sleeps, and what he eats tastes like

boredom. Sometimes, just for the sake
of his old meanness, he'll throw a rock

at one of them, he'll spit and curse.
But nothing hurts the heavenly ones,

who are mostly children. So he opens his anger
like the parasol holy men carry. Black, with razor

tips, it affords a split-second of shade when he falls
to the other place at the moment we unveil

the plaque with his life reduced to a dash
between dates, after we've kept him alive with kaddish

for a year, after we stood up for him
every Friday night. Then he will be with *satan*,

Hebrew for informer, just another crony
exchanging inside dope at the track. He'll hack his way

to the betting windows through tunnels of solid rock
while the tote board spins like eyes rolling back.

He'll hear the bell, watch the gate wheeled off
like a hearse stripped down to its chassis, and lift

his binoculars: in the infield instead of palms
and flamingos, a garden of flames.

And on the soft brown turf, print after print—
a stampede—but of course

no horses.

The Mystery of My Father's Cleanliness

How deep in the wood is the *sweet*
of the sweet-gum tree? On the outside
all you see are limp stars
for leaves, scabby bark and branches
going everywhere, like light.
Perhaps his cleanliness was like that—
a sweet sap that flooded his limbs
and perfumed his skin, because he never bathed.
Except for his fishing gear reeking and stiff
with blood and scales, even the clothes
in the hamper leaked only the tawny
scent of cigarettes.

Suave and dark when he was young, like Rudolf Valentino,
now he is a dry leaf, a corn husk,
the golden welt when you brush
against hibiscus. Now he is clean
as the grit-scoured shells on the beach,
now he is cold and distant as the stars.
But didn't he sweat with ardor once, didn't
his piss stink, his asshole, his armpits?
Maybe the rankness dripped into his heart,
distilled by some strange chemistry
that churned it into words and took away
his tears until nothing laved him
but his own pure rage.

Passive Resistance

I'm teaching those who will step across the line to be arrested
that language can be violent, too, as yesterday, when they
        taunted the guide
on the government bus tour of the Nevada Nuclear Test
Site, blamed her for the puddled aluminum homes,
        the re-bar peeled

off the bank vaults like melted licorice sticks, the craters that
        look like the earth
sucked in its cheeks and held its breath. I've given them a "box
        of words"—
"neon," "casino," "angel"—to keep their righteousness from
        bursting forth.
I'm reading them my own bad lines to help them over the hurdle

of fear. But I came to Las Vegas with a secret motive—to drop
        a C-note
for my father, one year dead. I didn't attend the unveiling of
        his stone,
not wishing to show him respect, knowing that under his coat
of clay, he was still a threat, that his half-life decayed into mine.

Last night I clung to roulette as if to the helm of some ghost ship.
It took three hours to lose sixty bucks. I bet his birthday a dozen
times, won once and pulled ahead. The slot machines rolled ripe
cherries into my lap. My father adored, in the sense of worshiped,
        this cousin

to Disney World, with its waitresses dressed as slave girls,
   clockless rooms,
automatic change machines, Glitter Gulch's neon canyons.
Racing form, fishing dock, or poker chips, he was always
   chumming
for luck. That is the gambler's lot—to live in the seconds *before*
   the dice run

aground on the felt or the racehorse pins the jockey's silks to
   the wind.
Now my students write faster under the plain-faced clock,
   cramming all
their passion into eight lines, using ten of the words which
   do not include
"justice," "bomb," "Nagasaki," or "atomic." Be personal,

I said—complicitous, not haughty. Imagine yourself on the
   wooden bleachers
happy to watch the desert lit from below by the incandescent
palsy of an underground bomb. Invent a science that could
   prosper
from 800 tests. Is evil a force or a lack, like the shadow that
   carves the crescent

moon? Tomorrow, they'll return to the Site, armed with hats,
   canteens
sunscreen and towels. They'll alert the police, tape their wrists
   for the handcuffs.
Tonight I'll lose the last forty dollars in a kind of mechanical
   keening,
playing the slots, craps, roulette again, games without a bluff.

I won't strew a bucket of chips on the floor to watch human

beings grovel, the way that my father would. I'll bet his birthday
   and deathday.

I'll lose without contempt for the gamblers, without resisting the
   odds, doom in

my emptying pockets as I near what must have been ground-zero

for him. I'll offer this peaceful protest against the violence he
   exacted

as his due. Let these be the last wages of Philip Steine.

Let them be clawed aside by the croupier, squandered like the
   origami

cranes folded in yesterday's seminar to nosedive onto the hottest

spot in the world while the disobedient cross the line.

Black Drum

At last the fish thrashed
out of the water
as if to break the black
bars on his side. One eye
felt the air, the dry

death of it, then he plunged again
in downward spirals.
We had been struggling for ten
minutes—a lifetime—over whose world
would prevail: his, with its purled

edges and continuous center, or mine
with its yin and yang,
its surface incised into sky
and sea, the land like a scar
between.

A crowd had gathered, you could sense
their excitement
the way you feel tension
on the line when something strikes.
You could hear the awe when they looked

at what I was battling—a creature
who belonged farther out, an ocean
liner in a backwater
bayou. My arms ached with happiness,
my sight narrowed to the place

where the line disappeared, the rod
bent to a hairpin, the fish pulling
at me like religion or god
with the strength of what can't be
seen.

Finally, like all saints, he tired,
he became more flesh than force,
flapping on his side, heaving for air,
the marble eye lidless against the sun,
the green water gilding the silver bands

between the black. I have not missed
my father since he died, but now
I want to tell him about the tackle, test,
bait, how the drag was set, though he'd disparage
my catch, remind me of the snook he bragged

of courting for seven years
by the pilings of his condo.
My father, gone entirely sour
by the time I was five, lived for
two things: the racetrack and the pier.

And I was nothing to him, I was only
a noise that shattered his nerves
a mouth chewing too loudly.
Whatever kept him together was thin and taut
as this line. Now someone lowers a basket net

to cradle the fish as we hoist
him to the dock, hooked through the lip,

a gash in the beautiful tail like a broken wish
bone. And there the scarlet blood.
I had forgotten his blood. I had

forgotten that every beauty involves a wound.
Now I pull the fish
from the mournful sound
in which he lived. His gills beat
like stubby wings, the red plush pleats

turning pink, all the fight gone
out of him. And now the fish
is like a man whose agony
was mysterious, whose every gesture,
every silence, was a roar.

Notes from the Sketchbook of Gustav Klimt

1. ## "RECUMBENT SEMI-NUDE FROM THE RIGHT"
    (Blue crayon on paper)

    She isn't thinking of me
    though she is
    making love as if that movement, too,
    were an extension of the patterned
    garment bunched up around her hips,
    something silky covered with circles.

    After she leaves I'll fill in the rest
    of the ornamentation—clamoring
    wallpaper, brocade house slippers
    on the braid rug. Now I trace the neck
    of a horse rearing back where thigh
    meets knee, the refusals in that muscle.

    Like a potter fluting wet clay,
    that's how she fingers herself.
    On the body's wheel, too, touch
    becomes motif so suddenly.
    If all of this were myth,
    I'd be the shower of gold,

    the bill of the swan clacking
    between her legs. Her voice,
    if it were visible, would settle inside
    these faint blue swirls, like words magically
    sucked from a page, drawn back
    through the pen's nib.

2. "ISLAND ON THE ATTERSEE"
   (Oil on canvas)

Boating on the Attersee, I was always struck
by how the clouds mimicked the shape of your puffed
sleeves or frayed to silky wisps like the rock-

swept hem of the kimono you lounged in evenings
after the sun had brushed the lake with molten
gold, then sank like a drowsy eye. The things

I imagined when I heard you rustle through the hall:
myself as the strict wood floor, your bare feet pressed
in a kind of kiss against each cell;

myself as the air itself, displaced by a little sigh,
by tendrils of warmth seeping from your orifices,
my atoms stirred until I was a genie swirling high

above your head, god-like, ready to grant any wish.
Until you wished for that false veneer—
until you wished us middle-aged, arm in arm a-swish

on Josefstadterstrasser, decorative and stiff
as that old self-portrait I used in "Shakespeare's
Theatre," where I lean toward the stage in my white ruff,

collared by the state, an artist on a leash only inches
long. Even then my gaze wanders to rouged lips,
the shallow breaths that strain against waists pinched

by whalebone. . . . But now see how the light assumes
the house, how it paves the lake, how only paint
can name these names.

3. "COUNTRY GARDEN WITH CRUCIFIX"
   (Oil on canvas)

Today, in a country garden
on the Attersee,
I saw a wayside crucifix
staked-out among the rows
of herbs and botanicals,
and climbing up around its wooden niche,
flowers throbbing in a springy tower,
as if a painter had blotted
his palette on the air.

Christ's body was the only pale
stalk among the massed, brilliant vines
and thick pigments, his loincloth
a wilted spathe that covered
his humanity. Below him,
on the same post, the Virgin,
rendered as she so often is—
as a blue curtain parted
by face and hands—ascended

until her hood nearly grazed
his sad, dangling feet,
until her blueness
pooled beneath him like his shadow.
The pair hung there for decades,
touched up, I'm told, with leftover
housepaint, his stigmata one year
barn-red, the next, scabbed over
with chair-rail brown.

And the Virgin also, her blue
variable as the sky,
darkening as if with an anger denied her . . . .
It was a lush garden bordering
a wood, its edges blurred with wildflowers.
A faint wash of blue seeped
between the foliage; stippled leaves
screened the vacant sky—a mesh
to keep the vacuum out.

I have always balked
at the purely decorative,
but then I saw that the symbolic
could stir us by its absence:
tree trunks set like monumental
vases from which spilled
casual sprays of branches
and leaves; the pear trees
in the distant orchard

like so many dropped bouquets;
and beneath my feet golden leaf
litter fluttering like stalled angels.
Even the Christ and Mary
reserved their long grief
like simple tubers
awaiting a place in the earth.
The pattern flattened before my gaze,
past perspective, into the infinite,

each petal and board
equally frontal, equally
monitory, no need for skulls
or writhing bodies, the pucker
of lust and excess
purely present in color
and shape, alive
from the instant a line
corrupts paper.

4. "SELF-PORTRAIT AS GENITALIA"
    (Pencil on paper)

I returned to the terrain
of trees and vines and Christs.
I shouted your name,
I spit it out like the cathartics
the doctor brought last night.
I said goodbye
to architecture parsing
the landscape into emblems
and artifacts. I no longer wish
to make the parallax
correction. I grow dark,
my skin dark, my palette
bruised with blues and misty
blacks, the gold of my canvases
tarnished. Come, Emilie,
to the daybed beneath
the studio window where day
will drape you like a goddess,
your torso intersected
with delicate scarves of light
as if with love's true
mutilations.

We will walk not in Vienna's
streets, but in the garden,
overgrown, lush, its green
tendrils clutching the civilized
flagstone.
              I grow dark, my mouth
contains the night. I

am the touch
of lead on paper, bone
on bone, all curve and opulence
beneath this monkish robe.
I am the voyeur who works
the blank paper until

it opens like a window
across the courtyard
where a neighbor woman
lets down her serpentine hair,
removes her petticoats and the rags
between her legs, then tilts
her head to one side,
as if no amount of thought
could bring her body back
from what it is. What
would the proper Viennese ladies say
if they knew that beneath
each colorful gown,
I painted first the pubis
as Medusa, thickly lipped,
a paralyzing stare
in that single dark eye
that is the entrance to the Maze,
an entrance narrow as this pencil.

A French Woman, Her Daughter, and Granddaughter

They are lined up by size, like vases,
on an oriental carpet whose paisleys
and garlands resemble a gaming board

where they are deployed, held captive
behind the delicate white fences
of tatting and lace that separate

the public parts of their bodies—face, hands,
neck—from the private. Under their gowns,
the real wealth, not theirs to give, tears and mends.

Did someone take them to bistros? Do the kidskin
carriage gloves—draped like shot
birds over the camelback divan—

signal a formal outing, or only
this meeting with the lens? In a moment, one
of the women will roll and crimp pastry,

the other comfort the child from whose sacheted
armoire this photo fell seventy years
later, when they auctioned her estate.

Now the little girl frets to a blur, the women pull
themselves up like flames, their breath caged
in whalebone, dangle earrings stopped like small

clocks as the century turns.

"Thérèse Dreaming" by Balthus

Perhaps she's exhausted from a day's
shopping in Brussels or Paris, each face
in the crowd a terrain she tried to scale,
her own face still blank. Now there is time
for reverie, in a room whose striped
wallpaper could stand for all our lives,
the marching away from dreams.

The empty vases nearby—one transparent
pink for a single bud, the other stout black
with the fluted lip of a matron—
are they the two halves of her life? Surely
the fabric bunched up like a giant gardenia
is less like academic drape
than breasts cupped to be kissed.

Between her and the undented pillow
she only seems to lean upon
a shadow has already begun to cut
the dark groove of her life. Above the white
crotch of her panties, which the painter has made
the brightest spot in the scene,
she shuts her eyes in fierce pinches
as if to undream the creature at her feet
who for now is a cat relishing his meal, his saucer
rendered only as milk splashed in the shape
of a dish. No bottom, sides, or rim. Her body
barely contained like that, delicious
against her will.

"The Lonely Ones"

Color woodcut by Edvard Munch

They stand apart,
the man in his formal clothes
the same black color as the sand
as if he is another peninsula

in this landscape of dune
and spit and expanse. The sky
is desolate, the grain of the wood block
translated into turbulence, a wind

that might carry them both
off. If there is a moon,
it has twisted itself into the knot-
hole of a tree, of the tree that made this print.

How much can be told
from their backs! The woman unbending
as she steps toward the blue-green doily
of sea, the man staring after her white

blouse and skirt
like pages in a book.
Not with bitterness yet, only longing,
his hands closing on air like the wings of a small

bird. If she turned
he would glimpse eyes green

as the surf, long red panels of hair
framing her face in a triptych. Later, he will

equate her hair
with sin. Now, he is one
of the trees on the shore, and she is the farthest fringe
of the wave that stunts what it feeds, receding from reach.

For the Women of the All-Female Bookkeeping Department at H. G. Smithy's

I think of them with summer,
polka-dot dresses and white
enamel jewelry, a petal
on each ear. The rest of the year
while I was in school,
they must have worn drabber garb,
but I never saw them bundled up
against a cold world, only displayed
like a bucket of tulips for sale,
their bangle bracelets clinking like laughter.

My family looked down on women
who worked, but I, a trainee at fifteen,
was in awe of the magic
wands tucked in their bags—
mascaras, lip brushes, pink-tonged
lash curlers that caged their eyes!
I loved their seamed stockings,
the way they turned
to check them, one leg slightly raised,
the made-up face set back on the shoulder
like a clock on a mantel.

And their clothes—tight
sheath skirts, Doris Day shirtwaists.
A silk scarf at the neck
like a snippet of lingerie inviting
a man to carry them off

to someplace besides the department
stores where they shopped the sales
at lunch: Hecht's, Woodward & Lothrop's,
even chandeliered Garfinkle's,

where the wives of diplomats wandered
in saris and pearls. The bookkeepers
bought the best, believing a French
hat might be the key
accessory to a different life. It could happen
anywhere—on a streetcar or bus, walking
the long breezy blocks to the office
and back, chatting with the men who visited
our corridor from Real Estate and Rent.

I loved them the way I loved all my teachers—
so that in memory they seem more
adult than I will ever be.
O Miss Dottie, Miss Helen, Miss Elaine,
ambition had not yet been given
to you or to me. I wish I could
remember you simply as women
who worked for a living,
not as thwarted pilots and judges,
not as perpetual ingenues
swatting at fate with a kidskin glove.

In the Granite State

Warner, New Hampshire

Dressed in rain pants, duckwaders, and a slicker
all from your mudroom, I slog with you in the chill
gray mist up your riding trail flickering
with red and yellow leaves. The stone walls
scramble along like tortoises piled up to brave
this clamshell of a day. Your favorite weather,
you explain—in a former life you must have been a grazer.
Neither of us believes in reincarnation, save
for the sort in your barn: rain and soil reborn
through timothy and clover as stifle and hock.
Still, I pray you live a long human
life, then come leaping back across these boundary
walls, the world hanging upside-down in karmic
raindrops on your braided mane.

For My Sister

Now she appears in a vision: draped
like a Roman goddess unearthed whole,
she's come to watch my grief
after all these years. Death,
that steady industry, has not aged her,
has not furred her though I saw her
ravaged body only moments
after the last breath. We were taking
turns, my mother and I, standing
inside the coma with her. I'd learned
her language there, the twitching eyelids,
the tensed muscles that meant *oh, oh.*
I believed I could stroke the pain
from her bones, my touch soaking in
like a solvent oil. We were waiting
for her heart to congest, for the cancer
to fasten sucker roots inside,
invisible as love itself.
Outside, frailty and thinness were the only
signs, like a tubercular
Victorian who'd never be cured, but unwind
instead like a skein of worsted, her children's
faces edging off her lap
like crocheted squares. . . .

Dusk is seeping down, coating
the statue with a violet pallor, a faint
garland of rot. When she leaves
she'll carry away the hair she's cleaned

from my brush. That is what angels would do
if they existed: sweep away
our enduring parts, save us a little
each night. Instead, she lives in visions
of statues, in the bridal portrait
hung above Mother's bed that tows her
nightly to my sister. There,
Beverly seems to stand behind,
not in, the snowdrift of her gown,
like someone who has inserted her face
in the oval of a carnival photo
without knowing what history
she stepped into before the camera snapped
her bewildered smile.

III

Most men have some hidden altar in their hearts,
dedicated to the fallen gods.

—IRIS ORIGO, *Leopardi*

Even if Kafka did not pray—and this we do not
know—he still possessed in the highest degree . . .
the natural prayer of the soul: attentiveness.

—WALTER BENJAMIN, *Illuminations*

Articulos Religiosos

Keko's the name of the statuette
with bags of fruit and money,
a gingerbread house that stands for family
strapped to his back the way a weight-
lifter's belt protects him from harm.
The shopkeep props a lit cigarette
in his mouth to give him

life. While he smokes, I finger
Mr. Lucky's *I Can, You Can't* powder,
cattails of incense, male
and female black felt dolls whose powers,
coiled in turbans, the blushing
clerk won't tell. I wonder
if working here she has given up God

or taken him back. Does she pray
for the daughter with Down's Syndrome
whose small hands grab like fish
at anything shiny? The child's eyes flicker,
roll back in her head, seized
by what the ancients called
the prophet's sleep. And she does point

to the porcelain tableau I settle on—
a saint and her petitioners at sea.
Caridad de Cobre's cloak, upswept
to a billow, could capsize or safely beach
the boat of storm-tossed men at her feet.

"She's meant to stand in water," the woman
explains, returning the sample to its fish

bowl on the counter, "like Liberty
in New York harbor." Meanwhile, and forever,
the sailors parry the savage
blue hooks of the sea. Such turbulence
it takes for their salvation, water
lapping their chins as the cash drawer
rings open.

In the Viennese Style

In the Cafe Imperial, they are bringing out
the Mozart cake with its delicate

pistachio crème. I've been watching the linden
leaves as the wind lifts them

into the streetlights, how they blanch, then darken
as if they are having an argument

with the tree. On the Ringstrasse, trams
wheeze past and lines of home-

bound traffic blur to faint septic streaks.
The scrolls and curves of the Baroque—

lush, gold-leafed, excessive—look like nothing now
to me but hearts stretched out

of shape, the way tonight the soloist
took music plucked on strings and twisted it

through brass. We had a happy week in perhaps
the only city where we could feel

our marriage healed when actually it was forsaken,
utterly lost, when actually it came

to this: we could agree on what was beautiful,
that was all.

The Separation

The last thing of yours I touched was the leather
jacket, for the serenity that marks all dead things
from a saint's reliquary to the ashes
of a fire. For years we flowed like water
over each other. Your hands were silver
as the starry edges of a door
leaking dawn. Other parts were plum-
colored, shaped to eat. All of you
smelled alike. I opened myself
without shame. We thrust our fingers and tongues
everywhere, professors of salt
and sweat, of the body's wet
flowers. Who knows why we became a stiff pair
of knees, when once we had been leaves rising
to the slightest breath.

Thistles

I'm wearing my sunglasses that intensify
color, staring at the violas in the clay
pot, their yellow and purple questioning
faces, and remembering the thistles
that furred the swale behind our house
in Tel Aviv. They were tall and tough,

with flowers like lavender shaving
brushes bleached to a dirty
pink. Striking, but not pretty,
like an evening gown in tatters
and later, when the tufts loosened,
a woman gone so crazy she forgets

to comb her hair.
                You smuggled
some seeds when we moved
to Florida, but none of them grew. Like us,
I think they needed hardship
to thrive, not this steady babble
of sun and rain.

I am drinking a beer and listening
to a sad song on the radio. Tears fall
without my will, the way it happens
when you are so full of grief
that it brims over if you touch
something beautiful or see a small

kindness in public. I am hardly
here, I am the "I" a leaf would have
if it spoke against the wind. The song
is that old one about an Irish woman
who loved an Englishman and was burned
at the stake. The hair on his head

like a golden sea, the fine blue
threads at her wrists. *O my love!*
O my joy! is the refrain, which I always
thought was the lover's farewell,
but imagine now is the woman herself,
already bound, queen of her straw

mountain. She looks out upon her last
day and sees not the assembled
crowd, faces distinct from clouds,
but only shapes, that correspondence that must be
what they mean by God—farmers completing
the curve of the sickles they lean on,

crescents of flesh above the women's
scoop-necked blouses, globes of red
clover glowing like coals in the fields
and now the halo that will bless
her, already shining as it rises up
around her feet.

Life List

1.

Pileated woodpecker, egret, Carolina wren
anhinga, evening grosbeak, little blue heron—
these are the birds you set like cameos in the lens

of my binoculars. But now it is you who are
distant and untouchable, observed from afar.
Come close one last time, into my focus: you're

in your twenties, you have not yet quit school.
You spend Sundays on fieldwork, crouched by a pool
in the Everglades diagramming the dances of waterfowl

dueling fish in the shallows at dawn, their beaks
like swords with pockets. Such formal grace to stalk
their prey—minuets and mazurkas slowed to a jerky walk.

Europe lingers only in your accent and the net-
like scar on one cheek—tuberculosis of the skin, caught
near Ashkhabad when you and your mother were freight

escaped from a train. But no, stay quiet in the Glades
counting fish per square foot along a killing grid.
Be the budding ornithologist, hidden

in a blind or taking our baby daughter
to the taxidermy room where she touched the slaughter,
the dry-cleaned death and brighter-

than-life resin eyes, and learned not to avert
her gaze. Two years later you dropped out, reverted
to the merchant you were at twelve. "I *like* to be cutthroat,"

you said. Hardness is a talent. There is skill
in telling half the truth, a thrill
in besting someone that science doesn't allow.

2.

Today I hiked Payne's Prairie, glorying
in the lotus pods, the earth braided
with gator tracks, the goldenrod open
like a hymnal. From the sandhill cranes wintering
on their flyway in the marsh, came cries
like splinters of grief. Then the flock rose,
shifting like threads on a loom, like roving.
I walked to where the gators cross the levee,
made the sound that lures them from water, the deep
tongue click of hatchlings or a rival,
I don't know which. Last July, yellow
lotus blooms—two feet across, heroic
as federal statues—commanded these fields to sleep.
Today their pods stick in the wind's craw.
One by one I've relinquished my grudges
against you, remembering the days we threw
plates and drove the cars dangerously
and stabbed the table with knives,
we practically had to chop ourselves apart.

On the trail home, a juvenile anhinga
was drying itself so it could fly again.

Vulnerable until its plumage fluffed,
it perched stiff as a trophy on a branch,
black sleeves outstretched, looking
like a judge crucified in his robes.
I don't want words from you, I don't want touch.
I tried to pull you from under beds,
out of the hearth, out of the barn where you shivered
for your life. Little boy tied
to his mother's pigtail as she fled, man
I loved more than half my life, I love you
no more, I wish you whatever you're greedy for,
just as I wish the anhinga warmth, a perch
beyond the gator's leaping maw. Poor
anhinga, also called the snakebird.
It has feathers but no oil glands,
no protection but this pose against
the wet world.

Hermit Crab

And here with no overture, no artifice
is the long-nailed hand of a vamp
fretted with scabs, each claw a finger
knuckled around a drink. The room is smoky.
The hand shakes. It wears a chunky
bracelet that like a tambourine calls attention
to the woman lifting her glass like a wish
to the light, thinking *cheers*, thinking her life
will always be like this: an instrument
without a plectrum. And orders
another, while men—some of them, too, like lanterns
left out in the rain—eye her, adding her up,
adding their musk to the perpetual dusk
of such rooms. To move

from one life to another, one must finally rush
after the long slowness, the ablutions
with glue and slapdash applications
of will. Even after the animal probes
the shell it has selected, it still
hesitates, awaiting the right wave. The sea
is in plenary session and votes to toss
it about. The woman swirls the good scotch
in her glass and licks the rim,
her tongue darting the way
the crab will when it scuttles
its legless, comma-shaped body from one
volute to the next. It lives tucked in, dragging
its shell across the bottom, carefully pressing

like a woman dividing her breasts
into quadrants, checking. This woman
could mistake anything for love, as once
when she heard the stethoscopic rushing
of blood and thought it a storm
instead of the body's ho-hum. Sometimes
the legs of the men look sturdy as columns
to her, sometimes they look like pylons
marking off a detour or dangerous course.
The crab is alone except when it mates
or kills. The woman recrosses
her legs, the rasp of her stockings
like stealthy steps in the dark
or someone walking on sand.

The Gene

I abhor this clapping of thunder,
the air loud and swirling like a drill
routing the tropical green.
I hate the verge
of damage.

And this war, always some war,
left like a razor on the sink
while God stuffs a shaft of light into the lake,
stirs some dirt into the heat.

Does the word "stone" give you a little starry
sensation? Do you know the blind vole
relishes the world through its nose and feet
largely as degrees of dampness and cold?
And you, dearest, what do you love?

Vigil without Words

After a decade of strokes, then three days
of grand mal seizures, you lie gowned
in faded cornflowers, a frostbitten garden
surrounded by hospital white.
The bed absorbs your sobs. You want to leave
for home, ready to die at the same age

as your own mother. Hospitalized in her dotage
after breaking a hip on her birthday,
she bossed the nurses, conducted her leave-
taking not in jewels and silks, but gowned
like you, in the regalia of illness, white
plastic tubes draping the ruined garden

that birthed four. We paid our last regards
to a machine. Now I watch old age
divide your body into parts like white
light through a prism. You're aphasic, dazed.
My voice can't penetrate the gown
of silence you wear even while thrashing to leave.

Recently, I've begun to say *love, I love
you.* But it's only love the way a garden
might be called an absence of weeds instead of a gown
of flowers and fruit. Look at us: eighty-two and fifty, ages
of silence between us! All those days
I cowered under the piano, wishing the row of white

teeth above me could bite. Father was like white
water, always raging, always leaving

us to play the horses. Even the day
he pawned your wedding ring and ruby ring-guards
you loved him more. I never said *hostage*
but paid your ransom with dread and prom gowns

prim enough to avert his wrath. He's gone.
Bad mother, I could say now, *coward*. You white-
washed his every cruelty. But we're beyond that age.
Your paralyzed hand curls in like a dried leaf.
The other presses my arm to your lips, soft gardenias.
I recognize the blank space you inhabit today

from the days whited-out in your closet, that garden
of shoes and gowns where I played at leaving, at aging
into the mother I never had. The mother I am for you now.

At Freud's House

In this city of statues, only a plaque
marks the spot: 19 Berggasse,
Sigmund Freud House. The famous
couch isn't here, but the waiting
room furniture—womb-red plush sofa and chairs
sent by Anna thirty-five years later—
is authentic. And the bookcases, still groaning
under the weight of so much thought.

Imagine that June night after the Anschluss
when he finally agreed to leave Vienna,
a place, he said, where he'd never
encountered a single original
idea. He arranges a few antiquities
in the indifferent moonlight of the sill,
the best of the little gods
and goddesses already crated, saved

this time not for the grave,
but his new life in London. For months
the cancer has made it difficult to speak.
He's learned to use gesture instead,
a particular bent of his head says *go on, I'm
listening.* All his life he untangled threads,
coaxed the story from the story
secreted around it, like a shell,

until he found the animal inside,
a soft legless thing that could not distinguish
punishment from praise and could not escape

its nacreous walls that shimmered like dreams.
He loved some of his patients—*loved*
was the word he used—invited them
to family dinners, lent money to a few. Why
should he have

refused? Even Moses was human. How else
could he lead a people out of a great injustice
into a greater wilderness?
Now late sunlight dapples the page left on his desk
to lend an air of immediacy.
Downtown, the bronze waltz kings tip
their hats, tip their hats
as if their music were still the rage.

Letter Home from Brooklyn

Through my window, asphalt rooftops, cyclone
fencing like razor-sharp curls of smoke.
Tonight, for the first time, I found the clock
tower on Flatbush in the snaggle-toothed skyline.
I'm trying to love this place the way I love
the half-formed odalisques in the Florida
sand dunes, the buttery sun. The first week,
when scarlet berries smeared the pavements at the park,
I saw run-off from an abattoir, raw public
wound. Today, prompted by the wind, I could
almost hear the harp of the bridge. I saw brick
buildings elbow to elbow like tweeds,
graffiti not as ruin but a place the light had loitered,
trying to form a word.

A Floridian Swimming in Brooklyn

It's cold in the municipal pool, dank
insulation pads the rafters
overhead. In my lane, linked
by bubbles, four bathers
circle-swim in the dark

of winter, season of change by slow
degrees, of the mile
I visualize unfolding length by
liquid length. Inside me, like a sail,
love swells and scuds. Six months ago

we hadn't even met. Now we're part
of the heart's elaborate
architecture, its cathedral.
We're the stone masons
who believed every join was a test

of faith. So you worried
about my first trip alone
to your public pool—a strange car
and the blurred streets, the night honed
sharp on sirens. *Don't take*

your purse, park near a street lamp,
crook-lock the steering wheel
to the clutch. At last I ambled in
with my cocky Brooklyn gait, though I feel
at heart I've been drop-

kicked into someone else's life—
a woman whose days are spent in the depths
of language, whose love in tight
black leather fills the doorway
now for thirty laps, happy

just to watch.

My Friend Who Sings before Breakfast

Lithium would kill him,
so Martin is healing
himself: no more poetry
or fiction. When songs approach—
music and lyrics crashing down the synapses
like big boats being launched—he resists
with a journal entry: *I like the dim*
neighborhood near the prison, my
windows full of inmates,
their numbered shirts
like so many price tags. . . .

He ratchets his bedtime back
an hour every twenty-four, the way you rotate
tires or crops, hoping
for symmetry even
in disrepair—Fibonacci, leaves
on a branch, this disease
shaped like a learning
curve. Still, some nights the air
will swell like a wave against his skin.
Last time he found a woman and gave her
all he owned—car, furniture,
every single book. Yesterday

he remembered what his father said
when he first saw him manic,
so incandescent with happiness
he seemed to disappear into it,
like the hottest part of a flame

that burns invisibly just above
the jet. Not "enjoy it while you can,
my boy," but "sing before breakfast,
cry before night."
                    Imagine a vise,
Martin says, in which you are both
the thing being held

and what holds it in place, metal
grinding on metal, that shining embrace.

Writing a Formal Poem the Winter after Your Death

In memoriam, Judson Jerome

Today the sky spun wire-thin strands
of sunlight as if to bale the snowdrifts like July
wheat. Last summer, a pump delivering
morphine through your neck, you taught formal
poems and read your latest work, your white
pompadour like a baton that stressed the time

of every verse. Meanwhile, on some clock the time
of your life ticked down to twenty-one stranded
days. Your head on the pillow, white on white,
you dictated bursts dazzling as July's
fireworks: a reply from the Dark Lady using the form
of the Bard, a memoir about communal life

and the ménage à trois that outlived
most marriages, a poem about timing
one's death for *Modern Maturity*. Depression was a form
utterly foreign to you. *Luck*, you claimed, *a strand
of happy DNA*. Two Julys
ago I watched you cast off frothy white

chains as you swam half a mile, white
corpuscles cleansing your blood, your liver
still good. The spring tides this July,
blue hooks of the moon, retracted the sea for a time.
In place of the water where you'd swum, the strand
lay broadened for miles, crab holes deforming

it like metastases beneath the skin. Formal
poems, you said, like sonnets, yield sweeter wit
and moral certitude. Rhymes are invisible strands
that connect the impossible, the way a pump delivers
the sky gushing from the land, its lever marking time
like a clock hand stuck on the moment in July

when I realized you'd be taken in the July
of your life. At first, you didn't reform
your daily routine, refusing death's sway before its time.
Then dementia did the final edit. While morphine whited
out the pain, you spewed venom on your life,
denied you ever loved your spouse, the child stranded

at the mental age of six. Now time serves up a posthumous
book wearing the white hair, a stranded smile. July
revised the formal message in each cell from *live* to *die*.

For the Stillness

We march lamely, reliably through the blowzy night
gaining only one tomorrow at a time,
no durable good. The beautiful
swan froths its feathers, and in the high plateaus
wildflowers release perfume from velvet glands.

Everything I have ever told you was under the threat
of death. I wore only the mask of life
like a bear denned up under snow. The cool fur.
O the fur like very dense mesh to strain
impurities from sleep and splay the first warm wind.
Such stamina, such strength!—as when the old rose
garden welcomes the blare of summer,
presses its petals in August's envelope
like letters from some hinterland
where the language is touch.

Like the jetty built to protect the swimmer
and the shore, every god is a form
of fear. Listen: at last even his song
is nothing more than an ornament
for the stillness.

NOTES

Page 23.   "Passive Resistance." Nevada Desert Experience is a group
          dedicated to the witnessing and nonviolent protesting of nuclear
          weapons testing. Several times a year they sponsor workshops
          and visit the Nevada Nuclear Test Site.

Page 31.   "Notes from the Sketchbook of Gustav Klimt." Section two
          and four are addressed to Klimt's life-long friend, Emilie Flöge.